from the Library of:

© 2010 Yvonne Hume
First Published in the United Kingdom, 2010
Stenlake Publishing Limited
54-58 Mill Square, Catrine, KA5 6RD
01290 551122
www.stenlake.co.uk

ISBN 9781840334845

TABLE OF CONTENTS

INTRODUCTION

This cookery book has been a labour of love for me and I have written it with great enthusiasm as my interest in the subject of the *Titanic* is very personal. My great uncle, John Law Hume, was the first violinist with the band on the *Titanic* and over the years I have become fascinated with not only this majestic liner, but also the food served on board.

There are thousands of *Titanic* enthusiasts, both here and abroad, who meet regularly. My recipes are aimed not only at these enthusiasts, but at all people who wish to indulge fine dining, without pressure.

I have simplified the *Titanic* menus, rather than elaborating on them, to encourage cooks of all levels to enjoy recreating these delicious dishes. I have extensively researched, tried, tested and fine tuned each recipe to bring you a cookery book that will support you in providing excellent meals, without disappointment. Every recipe carries a colour photograph, which has been taken from the actual recipe when it was freshly made, to ensure that you know exactly what your dish will look like, enabling you to cook with total confidence.

I have included napkin folding, other useful recipes, cookery help and advice plus *Titanic*-related facts, making this cookery book not only interesting, but practical and versatile too. With each *Titanic* recipe I have noted what class of restaurant the meal was served in and on which date in 1912, enabling you to get completely swept away with the nostalgia of this historic ship!

If you do decide to theme your dinner party to the *Titanic*, then please raise a glass for me:

To the memory of John Law Hume and all other innocent souls who so sadly perished on the *Titanic*.

Yvonne Hume

COOKERY HINTS AND TIPS

I hope that you enjoy replicating these recipes from the *Titanic*. If you are not overly confident in the kitchen, then please read the following ideas to help you to hold a successful dinner party.

I have found over the years, from cooking in both professional and domestic kitchens, that good planning, organisation and cleanliness is the key to success.

Always plan your menu to fit your capabilities; it is not advisable to try something totally different 'on the night' as the pressure you may feel under could hamper your success and knock your confidence unnecessarily. Keep your work surfaces clear by packing away all clutter that you don't need to use on the evening, especially that mug tree!

It is always a good idea to choose a starter or dessert that can be prepared earlier in the day, or even the day before. You can then opt for a more demanding main course. Where possible, experiment with the dish before the evening, this way you can cook with confidence and make the recipe your own, by omitting or adding an ingredient to suit your personal taste.

Make sure that your ingredients are weighed out carefully, prepared and ready to cook. It is advisable to put your recipe ingredients into dishes in the order that they will be used. This may make preparation a little longer, but it is a safeguard against missing out an important ingredient. It is so easy to forget something once your guests have arrived and demand your attention!

Once your ingredients are prepared, wash up and clear the kitchen ready for the next stage.

Before any cooking begins organise your outfit and set the table, ensuring that you have enough space left in the middle for terrines and dishes to be set once your guests are seated. There is nothing worse than a host juggling and fussing at the table to make everything fit. Don't forget to allow yourself plenty of time to get changed before your guests arrive. It is not very pleasant to turn up for dinner confronted with a red faced host who is sweating, flustered and a bit grumpy from the pressure!

If something needs to go in the oven after your guests arrive, use a subtle kitchen buzzer. This way everyone will understand that you need to exit their attention and do something in the kitchen.

All plates and terrines should be freshly washed and warmed ready to use. When plating up I tend to use latex gloves, this way I can handle food hygienically whilst also protecting myself from minor burns.

Having a glass of wine in the kitchen during cooking isn't the law! I don't think it a good idea to consume copious amounts of alcohol 'to relax' before or during a dinner party; it is so easy to either burn the food, burn yourself or take a 'devil may care' attitude and forget something important. Obviously, as the evening drifts along it is just as equally important to relax and enjoy your hard work.

Set up the coffee, cheeseboard, garnish, drinks and glasses and chill the wine. Open all packets and prepare as much as you can before the meal. Make a list of your menu in every small detail, to refer to if you get muddled. Once you go through this 'robotic' procedure a few times, entertaining will become a lot easier as you become more confident.

It is worth remembering that even experienced cooks make mistakes, so don't worry if you have the odd blip. If you do happen to make a small mistake or forget something, don't announce it to your guests; they will probably be too busy enjoying themselves to notice anyway!

Remember, a good dinner party isn't just about the food.

JOHN (JOCK) LAW HUME

When we think of the Titanic's band we immediately remember the saying "the band played on". To continue to play, when they were surrounded by panic and impending death, was a very heroic deed, one that I am extremely proud of my great uncle for doing. There has been a certain amount of debate as to whether the band did play until the end and what they actually played. My personal view is that if they had stopped an hour or more, as has been suggested, before *Titanic* slipped beneath the surface, there would have been time to put their lifejackets on. The fact that none of the musicians whose bodies were recovered were wearing lifejackets suggests that they played until it was impossible to carry on because of the angle of the deck. As to what they played, 'Nearer My God to Thee' was one of Wallace Hartley's favourite hymns and therefore that would make sense, but we shall never know for sure. It will be just one more of the mysteries surrounding the disaster.

After the sinking only three of the musicians' bodies were recovered; John Hume, bandleader Wallace Hartley and bass viola player, Fred Clarke. Of the three, only Hartley's body was returned home for burial in his native town of Colne, Lancashire. It was almost a state occasion with some 30,000 people lining the streets. Clarke was buried at Catholic Mount Olivet Cemetery, Halifax on 8th May 1912; his grave number is 202.

John Law Hume was born on 9th August 1890 in Dumfries, Scotland the first son of Andrew and Grace Hume. He had an elder sister named Nellie, who was born two years earlier in1888 on 30th April. There were a further two sisters, Grace born 26th August 1892 and Catherine born 28th June 1897. Finally my grandfather, Andrew, was born on 4th November 1901. It is no great surprise that John was talented musically, since his father was a music teacher as well a violin maker in Dumfries.

John was educated at St. Michael Street School, Dumfries, the same school that a *Titanic* steward in third class, Thomas Mullin, attended. Inside the main entrance of the school there is a marble plaque dedicated to the two boys. After John left school he worked for a while as a clerk for a solicitor, James Geddes, in Dumfries, but it was always the violin that was his great love. Some of his first public performances were played out between acts at the Theatre Royal in the town. Prior to *Titanic* John played on several ships, including the other great White Star Liner *Olympic* and at the beginning of April 1912 he had returned from a trip to the Mediterranean on board Cunard's *Carmania*. John was always popular when passengers had requests it only took him a few bars to pick up on the tune. Friends and fellow musicians from previous trips commented how he was always happy, smiling and eager to please.

After the sinking there was one act which almost defies belief. Black Brothers Music Agency, who had hired the musicians, sent John's father, Andrew, a bill for his uniform which included amounts for alterations and sewing buttons on. What made this worse was the fact that John, along with other musicians and crew, had their wages cut from the time the ship sank because they didn't complete the journey! Can you imagine this situation arising today?

As John's body wasn't identified until a few months later, with the help of photographs and descriptions sent by his family, he couldn't be buried in Scotland. He was buried on 3rd May 1912 in Fairview Cemetery in Halifax Nova Scotia, Canada, where his grave is no. 193.

Theatre Royal Dumfries.

On Saturday 31st May 1913 a memorial was unveiled in Dock Park, Dumfries to the memory of both John and Thomas Mullin. It is a sixteen feet tall Aberdeen granite obelisk that was funded by donations from various sources, including the local Boy Scouts. Prior to the unveiling, the Dumfries Town Band played 'Nearer My God to Thee'.

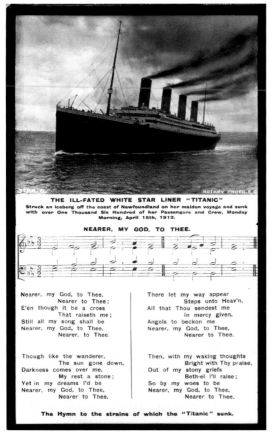

THE ILL-FATED WHITE STAR LINER "TITANIC"
Struck an iceberg off the coast of Newfoundland on her maiden voyage and sunk with over One Thousand Six Hundred of her Passengers and Crew, Monday Morning, April 15th, 1912.

NEARER, MY GOD, TO THEE.

Nearer, my God, to Thee,
    Nearer to Thee:
E'en though it be a cross
    That raiseth me;
Still all my song shall be
Nearer, my God, to Thee,
    Nearer, to Thee.

Though like the wanderer,
    The sun gone down,
Darkness comes over me,
    My rest a stone;
Yet in my dreams I'd be
Nearer, my God, to Thee,
    Nearer to Thee.

There let my way appear
    Steps unto Heav'n,
All that Thou sendest me
    In mercy given,
Angels to beckon me
Nearer, my God, to Thee,
    Nearer to Thee.

Then, with my waking thoughts
    Bright with Thy praise,
Out of my stony griefs
    Beth-el I'll raise;
So by my woes to be
Nearer, my God, to Thee,
    Nearer to Thee.

The Hymn to the strains of which the "Titanic" sunk.

A friend of John wrote the following and sent it to the local newspaper;

"Standing ready to disembark on the very shores of eternity,
the little band of hero musicians assembled for the last time".

May we never forget

Wallace Hartley, Bandleader and violinist
John Law Hume, First Violinist
W Brailey, Pianist
G Krins, Violinist
P Taylor, Cellist and Piano
J Woodward, Cellist
J Clarke, Bass Violinist
R Bricoux, Cellist

THE TITANIC

On Wednesday 10th April 1912 the port of Southampton was a hive of activity. Boat trains were arriving in rapid succession, from early morning, beginning with second and third class passengers. Finally trains carrying the cream of Edwardian society were pulling along-side the ship until just thirty minutes before sailing at noon. The embarking passengers were greeted by the musicians, who were split into a trio and a quintet, playing a variety of tunes but mainly up tempo. *Titanic* set sail from the quayside amid a carnival atmosphere before arriving in Cherbourg at 6.35pm for a few cross-channel passengers to disembark and more transatlantic passengers to embark. How exciting it must have been for those passengers to be boarding such a wonderful, 'unsinkable' ship. I know the thrill and expectation that I have felt when boarding luxury liners. On one occasion I sailed across the Atlantic to New York on the QE2. On the third day we encountered force nine gales; to feel so helpless and at the mercy of the elements was very frightening. I remember thinking at that time how dreadful it must have been for those passengers and crew on the *Titanic*.

Titanic leaving Southampton.

At 8.10pm on 10th April 1912 the *Titanic* set sail from Cherbourg for Queenstown, Ireland, where she arrived the next morning at 11.30am. This was to be *Titanic's* last port of call, where more passengers were taken on, mainly steerage who were setting off for a new life in America. At 1.30pm the *Titanic* then set sail again, this time for New York City.

At 11.40pm on 14th April 1912 the *Titanic* hit an iceberg that ripped a 100m gash in her starboard side. By 2.20am on 15th April 1912 the ship had completely sunk.

Out of 2,207 passengers and crew, only 706 returned, leaving a tragic death toll of 1,501.

The iceberg from the deck of the Carpathia.

It's very heartening to hear how many people are striving to keep the memory of the Titanic alive and there are numerous Titanic societies, both here and abroad. Conventions are held on the anniversary and thousands of like minded people enjoy getting together to remember this historic liner.

Millvina Dean, whom I met in July 2008, when she was 96, had been the youngest and was the last surviving passenger from the *Titanic*. I was due to see her again in August 2009. Sadly she passed away on 31st May 2009 at her nursing home in Southampton 98 years to the day from the launch of the *Titanic*. Millvina and her family were sailing on *Titanic* to start a new life in Kansas where her father planned to open a tobacconist shop. I feel that her longevity was perhaps due to the strong sense of purpose and duty to others that her *Titanic* connection demanded.

She was bought to prominence when Dr. Robert Ballard discovered the location of the *Titanic* wreck in 1985. Millvina very much enjoyed the interest that people were showing in her story and she went on to spend many happy years signing memorabilia, travelling abroad to conventions, public speaking and meeting *Titanic* enthusiasts. I personally found her to be a delightful lady who was no stranger to hard work, interesting and with a very endearing sense of humour.

On 18th April 1912 at 9pm the *Carpathia* arrived in New York with the *Titanic's* survivors on board, including Millvina, her mother Georgette Eva and brother, Bertram Vere. Sadly Millvina's father, Bertram Frank Dean, lost his life shortly after safely placing his wife and children into a lifeboat.

Olympic left, Titanic on the right at Belfast.

The *Titanic* was truly an amazing liner. She was 882 feet 6 inches long with a gross tonnage of 46,328, slightly more than her sister ship *Olympic* due to some minor modifications. There was a race for supremacy on the seas in this era between White Star and Cunard with White Star's managing director, J Bruce Ismay, wanting to have the large and grandest ships afloat. The same could be said of today's cruise lines where a year doesn't seem to go by without the "world's largest liner" being launched. Not all of the four funnels on the *Titanic* were from the boiler room; the aft most funnel, which is often referred to as the 'dummy funnel', wasn't used for the exhaust from the boiler rooms, it was used mainly as a ventilator for the engine room, the first and second class galley and the hospital on D Deck. This fourth funnel also served to give the impression of *Titanic* being even more of a leviathan.

Her top speed was 23 knots and she had 159 coal burning furnaces. She boasted 28 luxurious first class suites, two barber shops and a fully-equipped medical centre, including an operating theatre.

To keep passengers occupied and amused there were two libraries, a heated swimming pool, squash court and a much-needed gymnasium. The food on these luxury liners was superb and very tempting; it would take a very strong willed person to not over-indulge, and therefore a gymnasium was a necessity for some!

THE TITANIC CHEF

When Pierre Rousseau embarked the *Titanic*, aged forty nine, little did he know what fate had in store. He was head chef of three and held a position of great respect and responsibility.

Pierre was born and raised in France but after working in his native country for several years he moved to London to further his career. Whilst in London he lived at 7, Kennerton Place in the capital's SW district. He gained vast experience from working in Luigi Gatti's two Ritz Hotel restaurants in London, 'Gatti's Adelphi' and the 'Gatti's Strand', the North British Station Hotel in Edinburgh and on *Titanic's* sister ship the *Olympic*. It was working with Gatti that first drew his attention to working on board the new luxurious ocean liners. When Rousseau signed on the *Titanic* on 6th April 1912 he gave his address as c/o Gatti London.

His experienced background made him ideal for the position of head chef, in readiness to organise some 62,000 meals in one crossing. With Rousseau running the kitchens his friend Luigi Gatti was manager of the à la carte restaurants, where he had brought his staff from London.

The galleys were fitted and supplied with the latest equipment, but space was still very limited. It must have been extremely difficult working in such conditions, especially with the heat that would have been generated.

After the collision with the iceberg Pierre and kitchen clerk Paul Mauge made their way to the Boat Deck. Mauge managed to jump into a

North British Station Hotel.

lifeboat. He then pleaded with Pierre to jump, but unfortunately he couldn't; as Mauge told the inquiry "he was too fat". Rousseau's body, even if it was recovered, was never identified. Sadly Luigi Gatti also died in the sinking but his body was recovered and he was laid to rest in Fairview Cemetery in Nova Scotia.

Titanic **chefs:** P Rousseau, C Proctor, J Bochetez, P Mauge
Titanic **restaurant manager:** Luigi Gatti
Titanic **bakers:** A Barker, C Burgess, C Joughin, G Chitty, H Neale, J Davies, J Giles, S Wake, W Barnes, W Belford, W Hine

The logistics of food and beverage ordering, without the technology available today, would have required a tremendous amount of skill and experience. The elite of Edwardian society would have been very demanding customers!

The amounts of galley supplies are fascinating:

Ale/Beer	15,000 bottles	Ham & Bacon	7,500 lb
Apples	36,000	Ice cream	1,200 quarts
Asparagus bundles	800	Jam & Marmalade	1,120 lb
Bread (Loaves)	1,000	Lemons	16,000
Butter	6,000 lb	Lettuce	7,000
Cereal	10,000 lb	Meat (fresh)	75,000 lb
Cigars (complimentary)	8,000	Onions	3,500 lb
Coffee, ground	2,200 lb	Oranges	36,000
Condensed milk	600 gallons	Peas	2,500 lb
Eggs (fresh)	40,000	Potatoes	40 tons
Fish (fresh)	11,000 lb	Poultry	25,000 lb
Fish (salted and dried)	4,000lb	Rice & dried pulses	10,000 lb
Flour	250 barrels	Sausages	2,500 lb
Fresh milk	1,500 gallons	Sugar	10,000 lb
Grapefruit	13,000	Tea	800 lb
Grapes	1,000 lb	Tomatoes	3,500

The food was one thing but there were many other supplies including 57,600 pieces of crockery & pots, 29,000 pieces of glassware and 44,000 pieces of cutlery!

Beer waiting to be loaded.

courtesey Mark Bown collection.

Grand dining room, Titanic.

Dining room, Titanic.

LIST OF WINES, LIQUEURS AND SPIRITS FROM THE TITANIC

Champagne
Cliquot 1900, Pommeroy Naturel 1900, Moet & Chandon, Dry Imperial 1898,
Heidsieck, Dry Monopole 1898, 1900, Mumm's G. H.- Extra Dry 1900,
Perrier Jouet - Extra Quality - Extra Dry 1898, Ruinart - Vin Brut.

Claret
Chateau Camponac, Medoc, Chateau Rauzan Segla - First Quality.

Sauterne
Sauterne.

Hock Rhine wine
Nonpareli - Sparkling, Rudesheim – Still.

Moselle
Nonpareli – Sparkling, Josephshofer – Still.

Port
Old Matured, Fine Old Tawny.

Sherry
Vino De Pasto.

Burgundy
Volnay.

Vermouth
French, Italian.

Rum
Jamaica.

Gin
Geneva, Warrington, Old Tom.

Brandy
Hennesy, Martell, Frapin,
Liquer – Hine, Liquer – Frapin.

Whiskey
Irish – John Jameson & Sons (10 year old),
Scotch (11 year old),
Canadian Club, Hannis.

Liqueurs
Crème-De-Menthe, Benedictine,
Chartreuse (yellow), Chartreuse (Green),
Curacao, Kummel.

Starters

HONEY ROASTED SALMON WITH MOUSSELINE SAUCE
Served in first class on 14th April 1912

page 18

DUCK LIVER PATE WITH TOAST POINTS
Served in first class on 14th April 1912

page 24

CREAM OF BARLEY SOUP
Served in first class on 14th April 1912

page 26

OYSTERS FINDLAY
Served in first class on 14th April 1912

page 30

PEA SOUP
Served in second class on 11th April 1912

page 22

CABBAGE AU GRATIN
Served in third class, anytime

page 20

RICE SOUP
Served in third class, anytime

page 28

VEGETABLE SOUP PUREE
Served in third class, anytime

page 32

HONEY ROASTED SALMON WITH MOUSSELINE SAUCE

Serves 4

The honey addition to the salmon brings a gentle, but not overpowering, sweetness to this dish. I prefer to cook the salmon sealed in oiled foil to stop it from drying out. It is better to cook the salmon fresh, just after your guests have arrived, to ensure that it is not overcooked and tough.

The sauce will take just the amount of time that the salmon needs to cook, so this dish is very relaxing and enjoyable to make.

Remember, you can prepare the salmon parcels earlier in the day and put them in the fridge. The infused vinegar can also be prepared earlier, sealed and kept at room temperature.

This would also be a perfect light meal for lunch with friends, served with a small side salad and fresh crusty bread.

Ingredients

Olive oil, a small amount for
    greasing foil
4 Salmon steaks filleted and
    skinned. If frozen, thaw
    completely before use
4 Tablespoons runny honey
40ml White wine vinegar
3 Peppercorns
2 Bay leaves
1 Slice of onion
2 Egg yolks
1 Tablespoon of lemon juice
    Seasoning
100g Butter, cubed
150ml double cream
Spring onions/chives for
    garnish – optional
Freshly milled black pepper for
    finishing

Method

1 – Infused vinegar: boil the vinegar with the peppercorns, bay leaves & onion until reduced by half, set aside to infuse and cool. Strain and remove the onion, peppercorns and bay leaves; leaving the vinegar ready for use. *Try not to put your face too close to the vinegar whilst it is boiling, the fumes will sting your eyes!*

Pre-heat oven to 180 °C/350 °F/gas 4

2 – Rinse the salmon steaks under cold running water, pat dry and place each steak onto a large square of foil that has been brushed with olive oil.

3 – Pour one tablespoon of honey over each steak, seal the foil loosely on top of the salmon. Place into an oven tray and bake for 12–15 minutes.

**Make the sauce whilst the
salmon is cooking.**

1 – Put a bowl over a saucepan of very hot, but not boiling water. Add the egg yolks, lemon juice, infused vinegar, a good pinch of seasoning and one cube of the butter. Whisk until beginning to thicken. Never allow the sauce to boil.

2 – Add the remainder of the butter, one cube at a time, ensuring that each cube is thoroughly whisked into the sauce before adding the next. When all of the butter is incorporated, take the bowl off the heat.

3 – Whisk the cream until it peaks then gently fold the cream into the sauce.

4 – Spoon the sauce onto a warm plate and position the hot salmon into the centre, or pour the sauce over.

Garnish and serve

CABBAGE AU GRATIN

Serves 4

This dish may take a little more time to prepare than basic boiled cabbage, but once ready, it just needs 15 minutes in the oven.

You can prepare and freeze this dish at stage 6, which is always helpful. Cool, cover with foil and freeze. To cook from frozen; pre-heat oven and bake for 50 minutes, remove the foil then bake for a further 15 minutes.

Ingredients

1 Small cabbage, shredded
300ml Béchamel sauce (see end
    of recipe for this sauce)
4 Tablespoons double cream
1 Teaspoon of mustard powder
Seasoning to taste
70g Grated cheese
30g White breadcrumbs
30g Butter, plus a little extra for
    greasing.

Method

Pre-heat oven 190 °C/375 °F/gas 5

1 – Bring a pan of lightly salted water to the boil and cook the cabbage for 4 minutes, drain well.

2 – Gently heat the béchamel sauce in a large pan and add the cream, seasoning and mustard powder. Stir to combine.

3 – Stir in the well-drained cabbage and gently heat through.

4 – Remove the pan from the heat and stir in 50g of the grated cheese

5 – Grease an ovenproof dish and fill with the cabbage mix.

6 – In a bowl, mix together the breadcrumbs and remaining 20g of grated cheese, Sprinkle the crumbs over the cabbage, dot with butter and bake for 15 minutes until the top is golden and crispy.

Béchamel sauce

300ml Milk, semi skimmed is fine
1 Onion, halved
2 Bay leaves
6 Peppercorns
15g Plain flour
15g Butter
Pinch of nutmeg

1 – Put the milk, onion, bay leaves and peppercorns into a saucepan and bring to just under the boil. Remove from the heat, leave to infuse and cool for 1 hour.

2 – Strain the milk into a saucepan and discard the onion, bay leaves and peppercorns.

3 – Add the flour, butter and nutmeg to the milk. Put the saucepan over a gentle heat and bring to the boil, whisking constantly, until a smooth sauce is achieved.

PEA SOUP

Serves 4

This soup is not only very delicious and a striking colour, but easy to make and can be on the table within 45 minutes.

Ingredients

600ml Milk
1 Onion, thickly sliced
1 Large can marrowfat peas
10g Sugar
600ml Vegetable stock
80g Plain flour
40g Butter, softened

Method

1 – Place the milk in a saucepan and add the onion. Warm gently then set aside.

2 – Place the peas in another saucepan and add the sugar and stock. Bring to the boil and simmer for 25 minutes.

3 – Place the soup in a processor and puree.

4 – Push the soup through a sieve and return to the saucepan.

5 – Remove the onion from the milk and add the milk to the soup.

6 – Mix together the flour and butter, add this to the soup and thoroughly whisk.

7 – Bring the soup very gently to the boil, stirring continuously, until it thickens and is heated through.

Season and serve

DUCK LIVER PATE WITH TOAST POINTS

Serves 4

Pâté is a tasty starter that is simplicity itself, ideal if you have a main course that needs a lot of attention. I have suggested toast points with this pâté; if you prefer your dish to be rustic, torn bread chunks would be equally good.

Ingredients

225g Duck livers
1000g Milk
100g Melted butter
25ml Double cream
½ Tablespoon Brandy
½ Tablespoon chopped rosemary
Salt & pepper to taste
8 Slices of bread, crusts removed

Method

1 – Devein and trim the livers then place into a bowl with the milk. Soak overnight if possible. *This stops the livers from tasting bitter.*

2 – Heat 40g of the butter in a saucepan, add the drained livers and cook gently for 3–4 minutes. The livers should be cooked on the outside but a little pink on the inside. Don't worry if you need to cut into one of the livers to check if they are pink, they are going to be processed later.

3 – When the livers are cooked, place them into a processor and process until smooth. Alternatively chop the livers very finely and put them into a bowl. Leave the livers in the processor, or bowl, in readiness to add other ingredients.

4 – Add the brandy and rosemary to the saucepan then heat gently, scraping up the residue of the livers.

5 – Add the heated brandy and rosemary to the liver in the processor, together with another 40g of the melted butter, cream and seasoning. Process, or mix well, until smooth.

6 – Place the pâté into individual ramekins, pour the remaining melted butter over the top of the pâté (to seal), cover and place in the fridge to chill.

7 – Slice the bread to make two very thin slices. To do this place your hand, palm down, onto the bread and with a sharp knife gently and carefully ease the knife through. Cut the slices into triangles, place on a baking tray, sprinkle with olive oil and salt then bake in a hot oven 200 °C/350 °F Gas 4 until golden and curled up at the edges.

To serve
Place the pâté ramekins on a dining plate and arrange the toasted triangles or torn bread chunks around the sides.

CREAM OF BARLEY SOUP

Serves 4

This soup is an ideal starter as you can prepare it earlier in the day. Soup is always a good choice as it tends to please everyone.

In the original Titanic menu the soup would have been laced with cream just before serving, I feel that a half fat crème fraiche would be better as double cream can be so filling, especially for a first course.

Ingredients

1.25 litres Chicken stock
185g Pearl barley, rinsed and
    drained
1 Carrot, peeled and sliced
2 Sticks of celery, washed and
    sliced
1 Onion, peeled and chopped
2 Rashers bacon, finely diced
    Optional
1 Clove of garlic, finely chopped
2 Bay leaves
Salt & freshly ground pepper
4 Tablespoons crème fraiche
Crispy fried bacon pieces to garnish.

Method

1– Place all of the ingredients, except the crème fraiche and bacon, into a large saucepan and bring to the boil.

2– Skim the top of the soup.

3– Simmer the soup very gently for 1½ hours.

4– When slightly cooled remove the bay leaves. Place the soup into a processor or liquidiser and process until smooth, set aside.

5– When needed place the soup into a saucepan and re-heat very gently.

To serve

Place one tablespoon of crème fraiche into the centre of the soup then sprinkle with bacon.

RICE SOUP

Serves 4

This is a very satisfying and filling soup so only serve your guests a small amount, if you are presenting it as a starter.

As this soup contains parsnip, I like to serve it with parsnip crisps. Peel a parsnip with a vegetable peeler until you have fine slithers. Immerse them into cold water then drain well. Deep fry them in batches until they are crisp and golden.

Ingredients

20 g Butter
1 Carrot, diced
½ Onion, diced
1 Parsnip, diced
2 Cloves of garlic, crushed
90g Uncooked rice, then boil in
  lightly salted water.
800ml Chicken stock
30ml Light soy sauce
Seasoning to taste

Method

1– Heat the butter in a large heavy based pan. Add the vegetables and sauté for ten minutes.

2– Add the chicken stock, together with the soy sauce, to the pan. Bring to the boil and simmer until the vegetables are tender, approx 15 minutes depending on size of dice.

3– Add the cooked rice to the pan and stir to combine. Top up with boiling water if necessary

Simmer for 2 minutes and serve.

OYSTERS FINDLAY

Serves 4

This has got to be one of my favourite starters. Not only does it look impressive but it tastes good. If you don't like the thought of eating raw oysters, with the usual Tabasco sauce, or would like to try an alternative way of presenting them, then this recipe should certainly please!

Always take care when preparing oysters. Open the shells by levering the point of a strong knife between the two halves. *It is a good idea to protect your hand with a folded towel in case the knife slips.* When the oyster is opened, cut the muscle then wash both the oyster and deep half of the shell thoroughly under running cold water.

If you don't have a local fishmonger, any good quality supermarket will order the oysters in for you.

Ingredients

12 Oysters, opened and thoroughly
    cleaned, discard the flat shell half
80g Soft butter
5g Chopped parsley
20g Dijon mustard
1 Small clove of garlic, crushed
2 Slices of bread, crusts removed
    and finely crumbed
20g Cheese, finely grated
Zest from 1 lemon
2 Lemons, quartered, for garnish

Method

Pre-heat oven 200 °C/400 °F/gas 6

1– Place the oysters in a steamer, add the shells too, and steam for 3 minutes.

2– Mix together the butter, parsley, mustard and garlic then put equal amounts inside each deep shell half.

3– Place 1 oyster on top of the butter in each shell.

4– In a bowl, mix together the breadcrumbs, grated cheese and lemon zest.

5– Sprinkle the crumb mixture evenly over each oyster and bake for 15 minutes until the crumbs are golden.

Serve
3 shells per person on a bed of lettuce;
garnish each plate with 2 lemon quarters.

VEGETABLE SOUP PUREE

Serves 2

Soup is great as a starter or tasty lunch. You can make this soup as smooth or as chunky as you wish. Finish off with a spoonful of crème fraiche or a sprinkling of chopped parsley.

Ingredients

80g Butter
1kg Mixed root vegetables of your
    choice, diced. Include onions.
2 Cloves of garlic, peeled and
    crushed
2 Bay leaves
350ml Vegetable stock
2 Bay leaves
Seasoning

Method

1 – Heat the butter in a large pan and fry all of the vegetables together, including the garlic, for 15 minutes. Stir occasionally.

2 – Add the stock and bay leaves then bring to the boil. Simmer for at least 20 minutes until the vegetables are tender.

3 – Remove the bay leaves and pour the soup into a processor, in batches, until smooth.

4 – Return the soup to a saucepan, season and heat gently, stirring, until needed.

**Serve with croutons
and/or crusty rustic bread**

Main Courses
First Class

ROAST LAMB WITH
STRAWBERRY MINT GRAVY
Served in first class on 14th April 1912
page 36

FILET MIGNON LILI
Served in first class on 14th April 1912
page 38

CHICKEN LYONNAISE
Served in first class on 14th April 1912
page 42

MARROW FARCIE
Served in first class on 14th April 1912
page 46

SIRLOIN STEAK WITH
CREAMY MUSTARD SAUCE
Served in first class, 11th April
page 52

ROAST DUCK
WITH APPLE SAUCE
Served in first class on 14th April 1912
page 54

Second and Third Classes

ROAST TURKEY WITH GRAVY AND CRANBERRY SAUCE
Served in second class on 11th April 1912
page 40

IRISH STEW WITH DUMPLINGS
Served in second class on 10th April 1912
page 44

BAKED HADDOCK WITH SHARP SAUCE
Served second class, 11th April 1912
page 48

CURRIED CHICKEN
Served in second class on 11th April
page 50

JACKET POTATO WITH CHEESE
Served in third class, anytime
page 56

ROAST LAMB
WITH STRAWBERRY MINT GRAVY

Serves 6

I have lifted this dish with a delicious strawberry and mint gravy. There is nothing better than gravy made from the meat juices and fresh vegetable stock. I am sure you will agree that the strawberry and mint addition is a perfect finish.

This dish would be ideal served with creamed parsnip and potato mash (*see index*) or with griddled asparagus.

If you have any meat and gravy leftovers, place both meat and gravy into a casserole/oven tray. Completely cover the meat with gravy and seal with foil to stop the meat from drying out and this will ensure that the meat will be very tender after braising.

When needed braise for 45 minutes in a hot oven. Serve with steamed vegetables.

Ingredients

Leg of lamb,
    approximate weight 1.85kg
3 Tablespoons oil
4 Tablespoons finely chopped
    fresh mint
2 Tablespoons Boiling Water
2 Teaspoons Caster sugar
2 Tablespoons of white wine
    vinegar
16 Strawberries, hulled
1 Lamb stock cube, crumbed
3 Tablespoons plain flour
1 litre Vegetable stock, fresh if
    possible.

Method

Pre-heat oven 180 °C/350 °F/gas 4.

1– Heat the oil in a frying pan or hob safe roasting tin and seal the lamb on all sides.

2– Place the lamb in the roasting tin, together with the pan oil. Cover with foil and roast for 1 hour. Remove the foil and roast for a further 40 minutes.

3–Whilst the meat is cooking, place the mint, boiling water, vinegar and sugar into a bowl. Stir and set aside to infuse.

4– Hull and place the strawberries into a liquidiser, or mash thoroughly. Push the mashed strawberries through a sieve and add the fresh strawberry pulp to the mint sauce.

5– When the meat is cooked, remove it from the oven tray, cover and leave to rest.

6– Skim most of the fat from the tin then place it over a low heat on the hob. Add the stock cube and sprinkle in the flour, bit by bit, scraping up the lamb residue from the bottom of the tin.

7– Slowly and gradually add the vegetable stock, stirring thoroughly after each addition, until thick gravy is achieved.

8– Stir the mint and strawberry sauce into the gravy. Add boiling water if runnier gravy is preferred, strain into a saucepan, cover and keep hot on a very low heat until needed.

**Slice the lamb
and serve with a little of the gravy.**

FILET MIGNON LILI

Serves 4

Despite its elegant and perhaps unfamiliar name to some, this dish is very easy and enjoyable to make!

Filet (*fillet*) mignon (*small & dainty*) lili, is steak, served on a bed of sliced baked potato, topped with a Madeira wine sauce (*lili*). This is a delicious dish and one of my personal favourites. You could add cooked artichoke, foie gras and truffle on top of the steak, if you really want to gild the lily!

Ingredients

Potatoes
6 Large potatoes, peeled, sliced
    and put into cold water with
    a little lemon juice.
100g Melted butter, plus extra
    for greasing
Seasoning

Madeira sauce
20g Butter
50g Plain flour
285ml Beef stock
285ml Madeira wine
Seasoning

Steak
2 Tablespoons olive oil
20g Butter
1 Garlic clove, crushed
Seasoning
4 Steaks

Method

Pre-heat oven 190 °C/375 °F/gas 5

1– Grease an oven dish.

2– Drain the potatoes and pat dry.

3– Arrange one layer of potato, overlapping, onto the bottom of the dish then brush with melted butter and season. Repeat this process in layers until all of the potato is used. Bake, uncovered, for 35 minutes. Checking occasionally.

4– Meanwhile, make the sauce. Place all of the sauce ingredients into a heavy based saucepan and whisk, constantly, over a medium heat until the sauce is thick and smooth. Simmer, stirring, for two minutes and keep warm until needed.

5– Season the steak well. Heat the oil and butter in a pan. Add the garlic and sauté for 1 minute.

6– Add the fillets to the pan and cook until brown on both sides, as well done or rare as you require.

**Serve a wedge of the potato bake,
central, on a warm plate
with the steak on top.**

**Dot some of the sauce
around the dish
and serve extra sauce at the table.**

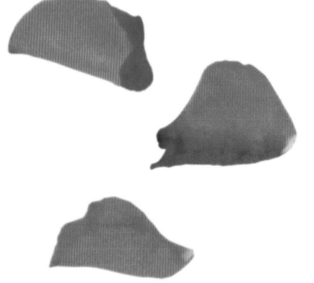

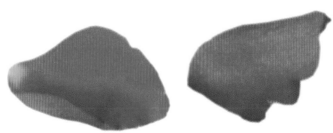

ROAST TURKEY WITH GRAVY AND CRANBERRY SAUCE

Serves 6

If you are going to the trouble to cook a turkey then it is well worth the extra effort to make the gravy and cranberry sauce yourself.

For moist tender meat force butter between the skin and breast meat of the turkey. I personally prefer not to stuff the turkey with anything other than an onion, lemon and favourite choice of herbs, which will add to the flavour of the gravy. Meat stuffing can be cooked, covered, in a greased oven tray on its own (*see index for stuffing recipes*). If you do decide to stuff the turkey cavity, always allow enough time for the heat to penetrate right through to the centre.

Allow 45 minutes cooking time per kilo of turkey from a pre-heated oven, plus allow at least 30 minutes resting time after cooking.

This meal can be served with the usual Christmas accompaniments, or is just as good with creamed carrots (*see index*) or an array of colourful roasted vegetables.

Ingredients

Turkey

Fat or oil for roasting
Turkey 3.0kg
200g Butter
1 Lemon, halved
1 Onion, peeled and halved
Small bunch of herbs

Cranberry sauce

300ml Water
100g Sugar
225g Cranberries
25g Soft butter
3 Tablespoons of port

Gravy

1 Turkey/chicken stock cube
3 Tablespoons plain flour
1 Litre vegetable stock, from
    freshly boiled vegetables if
    possible

CRANBERRY SAUCE METHOD

1 – Place the sugar and water in a saucepan, heat gently stirring occasionally, until the sugar has dissolved.

2 – Add the cranberries and cook over a high heat until the skins begin to pop.

3 – Reduce the heat and simmer, uncovered and stirring occasionally for 15 – 20 minutes. The berries should be softened and the liquid reduced.

4 – Remove the saucepan from the heat and beat in the butter, using a wooden spoon.

5 – Stir in the port and beat again.

Seal and chill until needed.

TURKEY METHOD
Pre-heat oven 180 °C/350 °F/gas 4

1 – Remove the giblets from the turkey and place into a strong oven tray together with the fat or oil.

2 – Wash the turkey in cold water and pat dry. Loosen the skin of the turkey by forcing your hand (*preferably wearing latex gloves*) between the skin and the turkey breast. Place pieces of butter all over, just under the skin. Then place the lemon, onion and herbs inside the turkey cavity.

3 – Put the roasting tin in the oven and heat the oil.

4 – Remove the tin from the oven and put the turkey in the hot oil, on top of the giblets if included. Cover the legs with foil and cook as per weight instructions above.

Baste at least three times during cooking.

GRAVY METHOD

1 – Remove the turkey from the roasting tin, cover and leave to rest.

2 – With the giblets still in the tin add the onion, lemon and herbs from the turkey cavity, throughout the gravy making. Skim the fat off the top of the turkey juices and place the roasting tin on the hob over a medium heat.

3 – Sprinkle in the stock cubes then add the flour, bit by bit, until it is incorporated into the juices, scraping up any bits from the bottom of the tin. *It will look worrying at this stage but the flavours from the giblets and cavity ingredients will enhance the gravy.*

4 – Gradually add the stock, stirring after each addition, until the desired gravy thickness is achieved. Add boiling water if a thinner gravy is preferred.

5 – Strain the gravy into a saucepan (discarding the giblets and any bits caught by the strainer).

6 – Simmer the gravy gently for 3 minutes then serve.

CHICKEN LYONNAISE

Serves 4

Chicken Lyonnaise is a simple dish to make. It is just chicken breast cooked in a pan with added flavourings. These flavourings are then reduced into a delicious sauce. Lyonnaise means from Lyon, France. The best way to serve this dish is with savoury rice (*see index*).

Ingredients

30g Plain flour
Seasoning
2 Large chicken breasts
70g Butter & a splash of olive oil
1 Onion, sliced
30g Tomato puree
1 Garlic clove, crushed
1 Glass white wine
1 Glass cognac
20g Sugar
50ml Chicken stock

Method

1– Place the flour and seasoning in a plastic bag add the chicken then coat the chicken completely.

2– Melt the butter in a large frying pan, add the chicken and residue flour.

3– Fry the chicken until brown all over. Remove the chicken from the pan and add the onions, cook until soft.

4– Add the chicken to the onions together with all of the other ingredients.

5– Cook gently, uncovered, for 20 minutes.

6– Remove the chicken and set aside in a warm place.

7– Turn the heat up under the pan and reduce the sauce until the required consistency is reached. Add a splash of boiling water if needed.

**Season and serve the chicken
topped with the sauce.**

IRISH STEW WITH DUMPLINGS

Serves 4

Irish stew is a hearty meal and will never cease to please. What could be better than sitting in front of a fire on a cold winter's night with a bowl of stew and dumplings, or returning from a cold sports night to this tasty comfort food?

Ingredients

30g Butter
500g Lamb neck fillet, cut into a
    rough dice
1 Large onion, cut into chunks
2 Potatoes, peeled and quartered
1 Large Carrot, cut into
    bite size chunks
¼ Cabbage, chopped
500ml Lamb stock
250ml Stout
Seasoning

For the dumplings
100g Self-raising flour
50g Shredded suet
Seasoning to taste
Cold water to mix.

Method

Stew

1 – Melt the butter in a large heavy based saucepan and seal the meat. Remove the meat from the pan and set aside.

2 – Add the onion to the pan and cook in the meat juices until soft.

3 – Return the meat to the pan, together with the potatoes, carrot, cabbage, lamb stock and stout.

4 – Add boiling water to the pan if needed; the vegetables should be just covered. Stir well to combine.

5 – Bring to the boil and simmer gently on top of the hob, covered, for 45 minutes, stirring occasionally.

Dumplings

Blend together the flour, suet and seasoning. Add enough water to make sticky dough. Shape the dough into rough rounds and drop into the stew, at stage 5, for the last 30 minutes of cooking.

MARROW FARCIE

Serves 4

Marrow farcie is, basically, stuffed marrow. Any minced meat will do, but match the stock accordingly. If one or more of your guests are vegetarian, you don't need to make them feel excluded from the dish; you can easily replace the meat with chopped cooked mushrooms and vegetable, instead of beef, stock.

To substitute meat: use large mushrooms and coat with olive oil, salt and pepper. Grill for ten minutes and when cool, chop finely, and add at stage 3. This dish goes well with creamed carrots (*see index*) and the colours are superb together.

Ingredients

5 Tablespoons Olive oil, plus a
    little extra for brushing the
    marrow
2 Medium onions, finely chopped
400g Minced beef
1 Tablespoon chopped parsley
1 Tablespoon Tomato puree
½ Teaspoon Paprika
200ml Beef stock
1 Marrow
4 Tablespoons mature cheese,
    finely grated.
Seasoning to taste

Method

Pre-heat oven 180 °C/350 °F/gas 4

1– Place the 5 tablespoons of oil in a large pan. Heat and fry the onions for 5 minutes.

2– Add the minced beef and cook, stirring occasionally, for another 5 minutes.

3– Add the parsley, tomato puree, paprika and stock. Stir well to combine.

4– Simmer for approximately 15 minutes.

5– Meanwhile, wash the marrow and cut the top off lengthways. Remove the seeds, then cut a slice from the underneath of the marrow so that it sits level.

6– Brush the inside of the marrows with oil then fill the cavity with the mince mixture – allow the mixture to cover the marrow flesh completely.

7– Top with the grated cheese, season and then bake for 55–65 minutes.

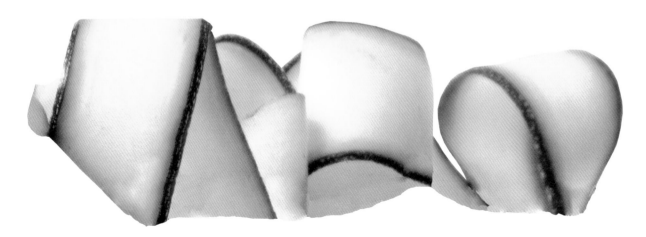

BAKED HADDOCK WITH SHARP SAUCE

Serves 4

This tasty fish dish is light and ideal for both vegetarian guests and those wishing to opt for the healthier option. It is very easy to prepare and cook and therefore it's an ideal dish for busy cooks.

Ingredients

Method

4 Haddock fillets, skin removed
4 Tablespoons cous cous
1 Knob of butter
2 Large mushrooms, chopped
3 Tablespoons olive oil
1 Garlic clove, finely chopped
1 Tablespoon lemon juice
Seasoning

Pre-heat oven 190 °C/375 °F/gas 5

1– Wash the fillets and place on a greased oven tray.

2– Place the cous cous in the saucepan with a pinch of salt and a knob of butter. Pour enough boiling water over the cous cous to cover it. Leave for 5 minutes then fluff up with a fork, set aside.

3– Place 1 tablespoon of the oil in a saucepan and heat.

4– Add the garlic to the pan and sauté for 1 minute.

5– Add the mushrooms and cook over a medium heat for 2 minutes, stirring constantly.

6– Remove the pan from the heat and add the lemon juice, cous cous and seasoning. Stir until well combined.

7– Spread the cous cous mixture evenly over the top of the fish.

8– Pour over the remaining oil and place in the oven for 9 minutes.

SHARP SAUCE

4 Shallots, finely chopped
2 Teaspoons tarragon, finely
    chopped
2 Teaspoon Dijon mustard
50ml Cider vinegar
30g Butter
1 Tablespoon olive oil

Place all of the ingredients into a saucepan and heat gently, stirring constantly, until the desired consistency is achieved.

CURRIED CHICKEN

Serves 4

This chicken curry is one that I have cooked for at least 15 years. It is perfect served with egg fried rice (*see index*). We all have occasions where a 'one pot' meal is needed and this fits the bill! This dish doesn't take too long to prepare and once cooked, you will have a pot of delicious curry ready when you need it. You can add a small handful of sultanas, or slice one banana thickly and add at stage ten, if you have a sweet tooth.

Ingredients

2 Tablespoons boiling water
2 Cardamom pods
4 Tablespoons oil
4 Chicken breasts, cubed
1 Onion, chopped
2 Teaspoons powdered cinnamon
1 Inch fresh ginger, chopped
2 Garlic cloves, chopped
1 Teaspoon ground coriander
1 Teaspoon Turmeric
1-2 Teaspoons Chilli Powder
130g Thick yoghurt
1 Tablespoon tomato puree
20g Butter
1 Tablespoon plain flour
400ml Coconut milk
200ml Chicken stock
1 Ripe mango, peeled and cut
    into bite size chunks.
1 Banana and a handful of
    sultanas, optional
Seasoning

Method

1– Split the cardamom pods and place them into boiling water to infuse.

2– Place 1 tablespoon of the oil in a frying pan and heat. Add the cubed chicken and brown (*no need to cook through*). Place the chicken to one side.

3– Heat the rest of the oil in a large pot and add the onion, cinnamon, ginger, garlic, coriander, turmeric and chilli powder. Cook on a medium heat for 10 minutes, stirring often.

4– Add the tomato puree, mix together the butter and flour into a paste then add to the pot, stirring well to combine. Add the chicken.

5– Add the yoghurt, gradually, stirring after every addition.

6– Add the coconut milk, gradually, and stir to combine.

7– Strain the cardamom water into a jug, discard the seeds and then add the infused water to the curry.

8– Stir in enough chicken stock to cover the chicken. Add boiling water if needed.

9– Simmer for 40 minutes.

10– 8 minutes before serving, stir in the mango chunks.

Season the curry and serve with rice.

SIRLOIN STEAK
WITH CREAMY MUSTARD SAUCE

Serves 4

Many people still opt for steak when dining out; therefore this dish will continue to please for many years to come! Served with this delicious mustard sauce, together with mushrooms, tomatoes and pommes parmentier (see index) you can't fail to impress.

Ingredients

30g Butter, cubed
30g Plain flour
2 Tablespoons of mustard powder
275ml Milk, full cream
3 Tablespoons double cream
4 Sirloin steaks
2 Tablespoons olive oil
Seasoning

Method

**Turn the oven onto low in readiness
to keep the food warm.**

1 – For the sauce: place the butter, flour, mustard powder and milk into a saucepan. Heat, whisking constantly, until thick and creamy. Remove the pan from the heat and add the cream, stirring to combine well. Keep warm until needed.

2 – Season the steak all over then put a frying pan/griddle onto the hob. Add the oil and heat.

3 – Cook the steaks, turning once, for just 3 minutes (or longer according to personal taste).

Serve

ROAST DUCK WITH APPLE SAUCE

Serves 4

Duck can be very fatty, so you will need to roast it on a rack in the oven tray. You can serve the duck with an array of colourful roasted vegetables, parsnips, carrots, potatoes, shallots and garlic.

It is always worth making the apple sauce yourself as it requires very little effort and tastes so much better.

Ingredients

1 Oven ready duck
    (approx 2 Kilo)
Seasoning
500g Cooking apples
100ml Water
1 Tablespoon sugar
20g Butter
15ml Cider vinegar

Method

Pre-heat oven 200 °C/400 °F/gas 6

1– Wash the duck inside and out, pat dry then rub seasoning into the skin. Pierce the legs with a skewer, this allows the fat to escape during cooking.

2– Place the seasoned duck onto a rack and roast for 80 minutes.

3– For the apple sauce: peel, core and cut the apples into a small dice.

4– Place the apples into a heavy based saucepan together with the water, sugar, butter and cider vinegar.

5– Simmer the apples gently until they are soft but not completely broken down.

6– Place the sauce into a dish, cover and chill until needed. Alternatively, you can turn the sauce into a puree by either pushing the apples through a sieve at the end of stage 5, or you can blitz them in a food processor.

JACKET POTATO WITH CHEESE

Serves 4

It is so nice to walk into a kitchen with the smell of jacket potatoes baking. Although this recipe is very simple, it will never loose appeal. Please note that these jackets will not work with microwave potatoes, thank goodness, a pet hate of mine!

This is a versatile recipe as it can be used for a main course accompaniment, supper or lunch.

Ingredients

4 Large Potatoes
4 Spring onions, finely chopped
2 Tablespoons mayonnaise
½ Teaspoon Chilli powder
Seasoning
140g Mature cheese, grated

Method

Pre-heat oven 190 °C/375 °F/gas 5

1– Remove any dirt from the outside of the potatoes. Place them on a baking tray and bake for 2 hours.

2– Wearing clean rubber gloves to protect your hands, cut each potato in half, then with a large spoon, scoop the potato flesh into a bowl.

3– Add the spring onions, half of the grated cheese, mayonnaise and chilli powder to the potato and mix thoroughly. Season well.

4– Place the potato skins back onto the oven tray and fill each shell with the potato mixture. Top with the remaining cheese then bake for another 20 minutes.

Desserts

FRENCH VANILLA ICE CREAM
Served in first class on 14th April 1912

page 60

FRESH FRUIT
WITH SWEET CREAM CHEESE
Served in first class on 14th April

page 62

APPLE MERINGUE PIE
Served in first class on 14th April 1912

page 66

BAKED APPLES
Served in first class on 14th April 1912

page 68

CHOCOLATE GANACHE CHOUX BUNS
Served in first class on 14th April 1912

page 70

WALDORF PUDDING
Served in first class on 14th April 1912

page 74

RICE PUDDING
Served in third class, anytime

page 72

SPOTTED DICK

page 64

FRENCH VANILLA ICE CREAM

Serves 4

Ice cream is always a good choice for the busy cook as it can be prepared in advance and never disappoints!

This ice cream can be made very easily in an ice cream maker from stage 4

Ingredients

2 Large eggs
140g Granulated sugar
480g Double cream
240g Full cream milk
2 Vanilla pods, seeds removed &
    kept, pod discarded

Method

1- Whisk the eggs until light and fluffy.

2- Gradually whisk in the sugar until thoroughly mixed.

3- Add the cream, milk and vanilla seeds. Stir for 1 minute.

4- Transfer the mixture to a freezer proof container & seal.

5- After 2 hours stir the mixture to break down the ice crystals.

6- After another 2 hours stir again, seal and freeze completely.

Your ice cream is now ready to enjoy

FRESH FRUIT
WITH SWEET CREAM CHEESE

Serves 4

For a lighter summer dessert this recipe is ideal. No cooking or setting time is needed and therefore it is very helpful to those who need to provide an impressive dessert, with very little time and fuss. This dessert will not work well made earlier in the day; the cream will leak and the banana will discolour. You can use any sliced fruit of your choice but below is what I find goes well together. The sweetened cream cheese is a good alternative to whipped double cream and worth remembering to use with other desserts.

Strawberry coulis drizzled over the fruit would finish the dish off perfectly. To make a coulis: hull a punnet of strawberries, place them in a food processor together with 1 tablespoon of icing sugar (*or mix and mash to a pulp with a potato masher*). Process until smooth, push the strawberry puree through a sieve then keep in the fridge until needed.

If you are in a hurry and need a quick sauce; put 3 tablespoons of seedless raspberry jam in a saucepan with 1 tablespoon of water. Mix and heat gently (*do not boil*) then allow to cool. When needed, stir and drizzle over the fruit and sweet cheese.

Ingredients

400g Soft cream cheese,
    half fat is fine
3 Tablespoons icing sugar
4 Kiwi fruits, peeled and sliced
12 Strawberries, hulled and
    sliced vertically
    (into heart shapes)
12 Grapes, halved
1 Banana, peeled and sliced on
    the slant

Method

1– Place the cream cheese and two tablespoons of icing sugar into a food processor. Mix until combined and creamy. Taste and if you feel that you would prefer the cream a little sweeter, add the remaining tablespoon of icing sugar. Alternatively mix thoroughly in a mixing bowl. Set aside in the fridge until needed.

2– Prepare the fruit and arrange the slices on the centre of the plates. Use a presentation ring if you prefer a neater look.

3– Alternate the fruit and cheese in layers, finishing with the cheese and a crown of any decorative fruit of your choice.

4– If using, drizzle with the sauce and serve.

SPOTTED DICK

Serves 4

Ingredients

75g Self-raising flour
75g White breadcrumbs, crusts removed
75g Shredded suet
75g Granulated sugar
150g Mixed dried fruit
Whole milk, to bind
A square of muslin

Method

1 – Place all of the ingredients into a bowl (*excluding the milk*) and mix together thoroughly.

2 – Very slowly add milk, bit by bit, until you have a very sticky consistency.

3 – Lay the muslin out and place the mixture close to one end in a long roll.

4 – Roll the muslin up, shaping the pudding into a large fat sausage shape and tie the ends with string. *Make sure that you roll the pudding into a shape that will fit into your steamer bowl.*

5 – Place the pudding into a steamer and steam for 2 hours.

6 – Carefully undo the muslin, dredge the pudding with granulated sugar and serve with custard (*see index*).

APPLE MERINGUE PIE

Serves 6

This pie is a pleasant alternative to the slightly sharper lemon version. It is just as delicious hot or cold, but is better eaten on the same day as cooking. Don't be concerned about making meringue; if you follow a few basic rules it will turn out fine. Firstly, always use a squeaky clean bowl and spotless whisk, if there is the slightest trace of grease the meringue will not whisk to peaks. Secondly, never allow any egg yolk or shell to be in with the whites.

You can use ready made pastry if you prefer then continue from stage 5.

Pastry Ingredients

200g Self-raising flour
1 Tablespoon icing sugar
Pinch of salt
100g Butter, cubed
Water to mix
2 Egg whites

Pastry Method
You will need a 22cm flan tin, greased.
Pre-heat oven 165 °C/325 °F/gas 3

1– Sieve the flour, icing sugar and salt together into a large bowl

2– Rub the butter into the flour with your fingertips, until it resembles fine breadcrumbs.

Apple Filling Ingredients

440g Bramley apples
40g Sugar
Juice from 1 lemon
1 Egg yolk
200ml Apple juice
2 Teaspoons cornflour

Meringue Ingredients

3 Egg whites
15g Caster sugar

Apple filling Method

1– Place the apples into a saucepan with the sugar, lemon and 1 tablespoon of water. Bring to the boil and cook over a medium heat for 4 minutes. Cool slightly.

2– Place the apple mixture into a food processor and mix to a pulp. Alternatively use a potato masher. Set the mixture aside.

3– Mix the cornflour with a little of the apple juice to form a smooth paste, and set aside.

4– Heat the remainder of the apple juice until it is fairly hot. Whisk in the cornflour paste and bring the juice to the boil, whisking constantly and vigorously. Simmer, still whisking for 2 minutes. Cool slightly.

5– Stir the thickened juice into the apple mixture and mix well. Allow to cool slightly.

6– Pour the apple mixture into the pastry case. Now make the meringue.

3– Add 1 tablespoon of cold water, bit by bit, stirring the dough with your fingertips for 30 seconds after each addition of water. The pastry should leave the sides of the bowl clean.

4– Wrap the pastry in cling film and place in the fridge for 15 minutes.

5– Roll the pastry dough out onto a floured board with a floured rolling pin. The dough should generously cover the flan tin. Don't cut off the pastry overhang at this stage.

6– Either bake blind by placing some greaseproof paper on top of the pastry base and topping with baking beans, or, prick the bottom of the case with a fork.

7– Put the flan case into the oven for 15 minutes.

8– After 15 minutes take the flan out of the oven and remove the baking beans and greaseproof paper, if using.

9– Brush the bottom of the flan case with the egg white and bake for a further 10 minutes.

10– Remove the flan case from the oven and trim the edges, slowly, with a sharp knife. Set the flan case to one side and prepare the filling.

Meringue Method

1– Place the egg whites into a bowl together with 2 teaspoons of the caster sugar.

2– Whisk the egg whites until they reach soft peaks.

3– Gently add the remainder of the sugar, bit by bit, whisking after every addition, until all of the sugar is incorporated.

4– Gently spoon the egg white on top of the flan, making sure that the apple is completely covered.

Bake for 45 – 50 minutes or until the top is golden.

BAKED APPLES

Serves 4

I have a fondness for this dish as it is the first dessert that I ever cooked unsupervised, some 43 years ago!

Make sure that you use large apples of the same size; I prefer to use Bramley cooking apples. You can, however, use eating apples if you prefer.

Ingredients

100g Mixed dried fruit
80g Soft brown sugar
1 Teaspoon Cinnamon
4 Large apples
50g Butter
A little extra sugar to sprinkle
over the apples before baking

Method

Pre-heat oven 180 °C/350 °F/gas 4

1– Mix together the fruit, sugar and cinnamon.

2– Wash, and core the apples, ensuring that all pips are removed.

3– Run a knife around the middle of the apple, just cutting through the skin. (*This helps to prevent the apple bursting*).

4– Slice a small amount of apple off the bottom to level and place the apples into a roasting tin. Fill the centres with the fruit mixture and sprinkle with sugar.

5– Pour a little warm water around the base of the apples, top each one with a knob of butter and bake for approximately 30–40 minutes.

Dredge with brown sugar and serve with crème fraiche, ice-cream or custard.

(*See index for ice cream & custard recipes*)

CHOCOLATE GANACHE CHOUX BUNS

Serves 4, makes 8 buns

I have filled the buns with a ganache, rather than just whipped cream to give a feeling of sheer indulgence and luxury.

This dessert is very decadent and takes a very strong-willed person to pass on this course! These choux buns would be ideal served with French vanilla ice cream (*see index*).

Ingredients

CHOCOLATE GANACHE

225g Best quality dark chocolate, broken into very small pieces
250g Double cream

CHOUX BUNS

125g Unsalted butter
300ml Water
30g Caster sugar
150g Plain flour, sifted
4 Whole eggs
225g Best quality dark chocolate, broken into pieces

Method

CHOCOLATE GANACHE

1– Place the chocolate into a large bowl.

2– Place the cream into a saucepan and bring to the boil.

3– Take the pan off the heat and pour the boiling cream onto the chocolate. Stir until the chocolate has completely melted and leave to cool.

4– When cool, whisk the ganache until it thickens.

Set aside in the fridge to cool and set slightly, until needed for filling the buns.

CHOUX BUNS
Pre-heat oven to 180 °C/450 °F/gas 8

1– Put the butter, caster sugar and water into a saucepan and heat slowly. When the butter has melted bring the mix to the boil then remove from the heat.

2– Add all of the flour to the pan and beat thoroughly.

3– Return the saucepan to a medium heat and stir until the pastry leaves the sides of the pan.

4– Gradually add the eggs, bit by bit, beating well after each addition.

5– Put the mixture into a piping bag with a 1cm nozzle attached.

6– Place large spoonfuls of the pastry mix onto a greased oven tray and bake for ten minutes, then reduce the heat to 160 °C/350 °F/gas 4 for 30 minutes. Cool on a wire rack.

7– When cool make a hole in one of the sides. Fill the piping bag with the ganache and pipe into the bun cavity. Alternatively, using a teaspoon, fill the cavity with ganache.

8– Melt the chocolate in a bowl over a saucepan of hot water, making sure that the water does not touch the bowl.

9– Spread or zig zag a layer of chocolate over each bun with a spoon and leave to set at room temperature.

RICE PUDDING

Serves 4

Comfort food in abundance! This traditional recipe is how my mother made it back in the early 1950's. She used a large bottle of sterilized milk, to give the pudding a creamy tang, together with whole milk. I have replaced the sterilized milk with evaporated milk. I like to cook rice pudding in the winter months as it really hits the spot on a cold evening. Don't scrimp on the nutmeg; it will make the skin on this pudding heavenly!

Ingredients

150g Short grain/pudding rice
25g Sugar
600ml Whole Milk
350ml Condensed milk
20g Suet or butter
1 Grated nutmeg

Method

Pre-heat oven 150 °C/300 °F/gas 2

1– Grease a large ovenproof bowl (20 – 23cm).

2– Put the rice, sugar and both milks into a bowl/jug and mix thoroughly.

3– Pour the mixture into the greased oven dish.

4– Top with all of the grated nutmeg and dot the suet/butter around the sides.

5– Place the dish in the oven, on a baking tray, and cook for just under 2 hours, stirring twice during cooking.

WALDORF PUDDING

Serves 6

This is one of the most famous puddings served on board the *Titanic*. It is quite filling so just a small amount per person with a spoonful of crème fraiche or whipped cream to the side will be plenty. You can add sultanas, soaked in apple juice, then drained, at stage 2 if you wish.

Ingredients

Butter for greasing a 2 litre pie dish
600g Cooking apples, peeled and
    sliced
60g Melted butter
150g Stale cake crumbs
100ml Whole milk
2 Eggs, beaten
60g Sugar
½ Teaspoon vanilla extract

Method

Pre-heat oven 180 °C/450 °F/gas 4

1– Butter a medium sized pie dish.

2– Layer, alternately; apples, melted butter and cake crumb. Make the crumbs the final layer.

3– Bake for 20 minutes, and then remove from the oven.

4– In a jug, mix together the milk, eggs, sugar and vanilla extract.

5– Pour the mixture over the pudding and bake for a further 25-30 minutes.

Serve with hot custard sauce, (*see index*).

White Star Line advertising.

Afternoon Tea

FRUIT SCONES

page 78

OLD FASHIONED BREAD PUDDING

page 80

FRUIT BUNS

page 82

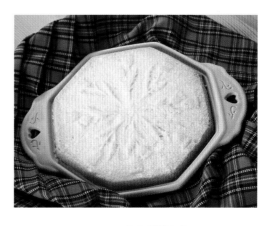

**ALL BUTTER
SHORTBREAD BISCUITS**
Served in second class on 10th April 1912
page 84

CABIN BISCUITS

page 86

JAM TARTS
Served in second class on 10th April 1912
page 88

FRUIT SCONES

Makes 6 scones

Scones are very easy and quick to make. To ensure a light mix; handle the dough as little as possible. It is fine to put the dried fruit straight into the dough, but if you prefer a softer fruit then cover the fruit with orange juice and allow the dried fruit to plump up for at least 12 hours, preferably overnight. The height of the scones is personal choice, they rise slightly when cooking, so gauge the thickness to whatever filling you are using.

Ingredients

300g Self-raising flour
½ Teaspoon salt
50g Butter or margarine, cubed
45g Sugar
60g dried fruit
Milk to bind
Butter to grease
Beaten egg to glaze

Method

Pre-heat oven 200 °C/400 °F/gas 6

1– Sieve the flour and salt into a bowl. Add the butter/margarine to the flour and rub in until it resembles breadcrumbs. As you are rubbing the fat into the flour; lift the mix up to allow air into the crumbs.

2– Add the sugar and fruit then mix well with a blunt knife.

3– Slowly add milk to the mixture, stirring until you get manageable, but not too sticky, dough.

4– Roll the dough out on a floured board until it is at least 4 cm in thickness.

5– Cut the scones out with a round cutter then place the scones onto a greased baking tray. Brush with the beaten egg.

6– Place the scones into the oven for approximately 15 minutes until golden brown. Check the cooking progress of the scones without opening the oven door.

**Cool on a wire rack, halve and
serve filled with cream and jam (*see index*).**

OLD FASHIONED BREAD PUDDING

Serves 4/6

Ingredients

225g White bread, crusts removed
300ml Whole milk
175g Dried fruit
50g Shredded suet
60g Granulated sugar
2 Tablespoons mixed spice
1 Large egg, beaten
Butter for greasing

Method

Pre-heat oven 180 °C/350 °F/gas 4

1– Butter an 850ml loaf tin.

2– Place the bread into a bowl and pour the milk over the top. Beat it until it is lump free.

3– Add all of the other ingredients to the bread and mix well.

4– Pour into the greased tin and bake, covered with greased foil, for 1 hour

5– Remove the foil and bake for a further 50 minutes.

**Turn out onto a cooling rack,
dredge with sugar and serve.**

FRUIT BUNS

Makes approximately 15 buns

Ingredients

600g White bread flour
125g Butter
125g Caster sugar
300g Mixed fruit
2 teaspoons mixed spice
Large pinch of salt
7g Fast action dried yeast
300ml Warm whole milk
1 Medium egg, beaten
Butter for greasing

For the glaze
4 Tablespoons caster sugar mixed together with 4 tablespoons of cold water

Method

Pre-heat oven 200 °C/400 °F/gas6

1– Sieve the flour into a large bowl and rub in the butter until it resembles breadcrumbs.

2– Add to the bowl: caster sugar, mixed fruit, spice, salt and yeast.

3– Combine the egg and milk and pour slowly, stirring, into the mix until it resembles soft but not sticky dough.

4– Turn the dough onto a floured board and knead for 8 minutes until it is elastic in texture.

5– Divide the dough into ball shaped pieces and put onto a greased baking sheet. Cover with oiled cling film and leave to prove in a warm place.

6– When the buns have approximately doubled in size place them in the oven and bake for 20 minutes. They should be risen and golden.

7– Carefully place the buns on a wire cooling rack.

8– For the glaze: place the remaining caster sugar and water into a saucepan. Bring to the boil and simmer, stirring, until the mixture resembles syrup.

Brush the hot glaze over each bun and serve.

ALL BUTTER SHORTBREAD BISCUITS

Makes 8 triangles

These traditional buttery biscuits are very hard to resist! They are ideal with a bowl of strawberries and cream on a summer's day.

Ingredients

150g Plain flour
50g Cornflour
100g Butter
50g Caster sugar
A little cornflour for dusting the inside of a shortbread mould.
(A mould is not essential)

Method

Pre-heat oven 170 °C/325 °F/gas 3

1– Sieve the flour into a mixing bowl and add the butter and sugar.

2– Rub the flour into the butter and sugar then turn out onto a floured board. Knead until smooth. Don't be tempted to add any liquid at this stage; the mixture will bind together slightly with kneading.

3– Lightly grease and dust the inside of a shortbread mould and press the dough into it with your knuckles. Leave the dough to set for 15 minutes. If you don't have a mould just roll out the dough into a circle, then crimp the edges.

4– Place the dough very carefully onto a greased baking tray or place the oven safe mould on a baking tray.

5– Bake for 25–35 minutes.

6– Remove the shortbread from the oven and with a sharp knife, mark the round into 8 slices but do not cut through.

7– Cool on a wire tray. When completely cool, dredge with caster sugar and cut into 8 triangles.

Keep in an airtight container.

CABIN BISCUITS

Makes 20 biscuits

These biscuits are an interesting texture and a nice alternative for those wanting a biscuit with a difference. I made the biscuits in the picture with half fat butter and semi-skimmed milk. It all helps!

Ingredients

115g Whole wheat flour
135g Plain flour
15g Baking powder
55g Butter, plus some for greasing
180g Granulated sugar
150ml Milk

Method

Pre-heat oven 220 °C/400 °F/gas 6

1 – Sieve both flours and baking powder into a large bowl.

2 – Add the butter to the flour and rub in to make fine breadcrumbs.

3 – Add the sugar and then add enough milk to make a firm mixture.

4 – Roll the biscuits out onto a floured board and cut into rounds. Alternatively, shape into biscuit rounds with your hands.

5 – Place the biscuits on a greased baking tray and bake for 15 minutes.

6 – Cool on a wire rack then dredge with sugar.

JAM TARTS

Makes 12 tarts

J am tarts are incredibly simple to make and such a pretty addition to a cake stand. You can fill them with either jam or lemon curd (*see index*).

When making pastry always work as quickly as possible, to stop the pastry dough getting warm. Always pop the pastry dough into the fridge, wrapped in cling film, to cool before rolling out.

When the tarts are cooked, remember the jam will be very hot and could painfully scald the roof of the mouth.

Ingredients

200g Self-raising flour, plus
    extra for dusting.
2 Tablespoons icing sugar
Pinch of salt
100g Butter, cubed
Water, in a jug, to mix
2 Egg whites
260g Jam for filling tartlet cases

Method

Pre-heat oven 200 °C/400 °F/gas 6

1– Sieve the flour, icing sugar and salt into a large bowl.

2– Add the butter and rub into the flour as quickly as possible until the mixture resembles fine breadcrumbs.

3– Add approximately 1 tablespoon of cold water to the mixture and stir with your fingertips for at least 30 seconds. Don't be tempted to add too much water. Continue this process until you have a smooth, non sticky, pastry dough. The dough should leave the sides of the bowl clean. Wrap the dough in cling film and place into the fridge for 30 minutes.

4– Meanwhile; grease a tartlet tin and flour the pastry rolling area and rolling pin.

5– Take the pastry out of the fridge and roll it out. Do not roll it too thin – otherwise the tartlets will be crisp and fragile to work with.

6– With a fluted cutter, cut out enough circles to fill the tartlet tin.

7– Press the circles gently and evenly into the tartlet tin and prick the bottom of the cases with a fork.

8– Brush the bottom of each tartlet case with egg white. This will help seal the bottom of the case. Then bake for 8 minutes.

9– Remove the tin from the oven and half fill each pastry case with jam (*see index*) and return to the oven for 5 minutes.

**Serve hot with cream, custard (*see index*)
or just on their own.**

SWEET ACCOMPANIMENTS

Strawberry Jam

page 92

Lemon and Orange Curd

page 94

Custard Sauce

page 96

STRAWBERRY JAM

Makes approximately 1.2L

Ingredients

900g Strawberries, hulled but
left whole
1kg Sugar with pectin
Juice of ½ lemon

Method

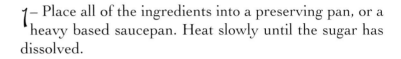

1– Place all of the ingredients into a preserving pan, or a heavy based saucepan. Heat slowly until the sugar has dissolved.

2– Bring to the boil and simmer until the jam reaches setting point. (105 °C on a sugar thermometer).

3– Cool then pour into clean jars.

LEMON AND ORANGE CURD

Makes approximately 575g curd

Ingredients

4 Medium lemons – for orange
curd use 3 oranges
125g Butter
4 Egg yolks
350g Caster sugar – for orange
curd use 300g

Method

1– Zest and juice the lemons/oranges and put into a bowl.

2– Cut the butter into small cubes and place into the bowl.

3– Beat the eggs and add them to the bowl, together with the sugar and stir.

4– Stand the bowl over a pan of simmering water and stir the mixture until the sugar has dissolved.

5– Without allowing the mixture to boil; heat through gently for approximately 2 minutes until the curd becomes thickened. It should coat the back of a spoon.

6– Sieve the curd, then once cooled, pour into clean jam pots and store in the fridge until needed.

**The lemon curd should keep, refrigerated,
for approximately two weeks.**

For lime curd, replace the lemons with limes.

CUSTARD SAUCE

Serves 4

Ingredients

600ml Milk, full cream
1 Vanilla pod, split lengthways
6 Egg yolks
35g Sugar

Method

1 – Put the milk, together with the vanilla pod, into a saucepan and heat until the milk is just warm, not hot. Set aside.

2 – Place the egg yolks and sugar into a bowl and whisk together to combine. Sit the bowl over a saucepan of gently simmering water. Don't let the bowl touch the water.

3 – Whisk the eggs and sugar constantly whilst slowly adding the warm milk.

4 – Now that the milk is incorporated, stir the custard over the pan of water until it thickens. Never allow the custard to boil as otherwise it could curdle.

Strain the custard into a warm jug and serve.

SAVOURY ACCOMPANIMENTS

PARSNIP AND POTATO MASH
Served in first class on 14th April 1912
page 108

CREAMED CARROTS
Served in first class on 14th April 1912
page 110

POMMES PARMENTIER
Served in first class on 14th April 1912
page 120

SAVOURY RICE
Served in second class 11th April 1912
page 100

CRISPY ROAST POTATOES
Served in second class on 11th April 1912
page 122

CRUSTY ROLLS
page 102

FRENCH DRESSING

page 104

MANGO CHUTNEY

page 106

BREAD SAUCE

page 112

MAYONNAISE

page 118

APRICOT AND RAISIN STUFFING

page 114

SAGE AND ONION STUFFING

page 116

SAVOURY RICE

Serves 4

Rice, on its own, can be quite bland. Therefore I have bought the rice up-to-date by adding eggs and spring onions. When the cooked rice is frying it is very important not to add more oil or the rice will soak up the oil and become very stodgy.

Either serve hot with a main dish, or cold, pressed into individual food rings, great as an accompaniment to cold meats and salad.

Ingredients

25ml Olive oil
2 Large eggs, lightly beaten with
    a fork
2 Spring onions, finely chopped
250g Rice that has been boiled
    in lightly salted water,
    rinsed, cooled then covered
    in the fridge until needed.
Seasoning to taste

Method

1– Heat the oil in a large frying pan until hot, but not smoking.

2– Mix the spring onions together with the egg and pour into the hot oil.

3– Rapidly stir the egg with a wooden spoon until it is just beginning to set.

4– Add the cold rice then stir until the mixture is well combined.

5– When the rice mixture is thoroughly heated through, season and serve.

CRUSTY ROLLS

Makes approximately 10 small rolls

Ingredients

650g White bread flour
1 Teaspoon Sugar
1 Teaspoon Salt
15g Lard
7g Dried yeast
400ml Warm water

Method

Pre-heat oven 230 °C/450 °F/gas 8

1– Grease a large baking tray.

2– Put the flour, sugar, salt and lard into a large bowl and mix.

3– Rub the lard into the flour, then sprinkle in the yeast and mix.

4– Add the warm water to the flour and mix well until a soft dough is achieved.

5– Knead the dough for at least 10 minutes on a floured surface.

6– Take pieces of the dough, roll them into balls (*approx half the size of a roll*) then place the dough balls onto the baking sheet. Alternatively put small pieces of the dough into greased mini loaf tins.

7– Cover the rolls with cling film and put them into a warm place until risen and doubled in size.

8– Remove the cling film and bake the rolls for approximately 15 minutes.

Cool on a wire rack and serve

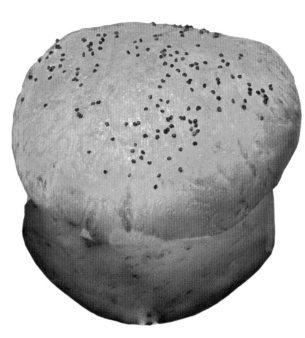

FRENCH DRESSING & SALAD CREAM

FRENCH DRESSING

1 Teaspoon Dijon mustard
Large pinch caster sugar
1 Tablespoon white wine vinegar
90ml Olive oil

Shake all of the ingredients together in a jar.

Serve immediately.

SALAD CREAM

2 Teaspoons white wine vinegar
1 Tablespoon of made mustard
142ml Single cream
Pinch of cayenne pepper
Large pinch caster sugar
Seasoning

Thoroughly mix all of the ingredients together in a bowl, cover and chill for 12 hours.

MANGO CHUTNEY

Makes approximately 865g

Ingredients

2 Large ripe mangoes, peeled and diced

2 Cooking apples, peeled and chopped

125g Seedless raisins

2 Onions, peeled and chopped

1 Teaspoon ground ginger

350g Brown sugar

2 Cloves garlic, peeled and crushed

½ Teaspoon salt

Method

1– Place all of the ingredients into a heavy based saucepan, bring to the boil, uncovered, then simmer for 45 minutes, stirring occasionally.

2– Leave the chutney to cool then transfer to clean jars. Once opened, store in the fridge and use within three weeks.

PARSNIP AND POTATO MASH

Serves 4

This dish goes well with so many dishes and is a good alternative to ordinary mashed potato. It is very quick, easy to make and can be prepared earlier, which is always helpful. Cook, then when needed just seal and steam gently, or microwave on medium power, until piping hot.

Ingredients

250g Potatoes
250g Parsnips
1 Tablespoon Crème fraiche
1 Garlic clove, crushed
½ Teaspoon nutmeg
Black pepper

Method

1– Peel the potatoes and parsnips, removing the woody core from the parsnips. Cut both the potatoes and parsnips into small chunks, then place the potatoes into one bowl of cold water and the parsnips into another.

2– Bring a large saucepan of salted water to the boil and add just the potatoes. After 5 minutes add the parsnips and cook together until tender enough to mash.

3– Meanwhile put the crème fraiche, garlic and nutmeg into a small saucepan and heat gently, stirring occasionally. Cook gently for 5 minutes ensuring that the cream does not burn.

4– When the parsnips and potatoes are tender, drain then either mash or push them through a ricer. Return the mash back into the saucepan and place over a very low heat for 1 minute.

5– Remove the mash from the heat then stir in the crème fraiche mixture.

Serve, sprinkled with freshly milled black pepper.

CREAMED CARROTS

Serves 2

This is a very good way of presenting carrots. Not only do they taste good but they have an excellent colour to enhance the presentation of your dish, especially topped with chopped chives or freshly milled black pepper.

This dish can be prepared earlier in the day, cooled then sealed. When needed; gently reheat, covered, either in a steamer or on medium power in a microwave.

Ingredients

500g Carrots, cut into small circles
1 Cinnamon stick
1 Tablespoon Crème fraiche or
    double cream
½ Teaspoon Lemon juice
4 Spring onions, very finely chopped
1 Teaspoon lemon juice
½ Teaspoon nutmeg
15g Butter
Seasoning to taste

Method

1– Bring a pan of lightly salted water to the boil.

2– Add the carrots and cinnamon stick. Boil until the carrots are soft.

3– Drain the carrots and remove the cinnamon stick.

4– Either mash the carrots, or push them through a ricer, then place into a large bowl.

5– Place the crème fraiche into a small saucepan together with the spring onions and gently heat through. Add to the carrots, bit by bit, until you reach the required texture of your mash.

6– Add the lemon juice, nutmeg and butter. Season to taste and serve.

BREAD SAUCE

Ingredients

300ml Whole milk
1 Large onion, halved
6 Cloves
6 Peppercorns
1 Bay leaf
½ Teaspoon nutmeg
80g White breadcrumbs, crusts
    removed
25g Butter
2 Tablespoons double cream
    (optional)
Seasoning

Method

1– Pour the milk into a saucepan together with the onion, cloves, peppercorns, bay leaf and nutmeg. Bring to just under the boil then leave to infuse, covered, for 1 hour.

2– Strain the milk into a bowl and discard the onions, cloves, peppercorns and bay leaf.

3– Add the breadcrumbs to the milk and leave to infuse for a further 30 minutes.

4– When required, gently heat the sauce through then stir in the butter, cream and seasoning.

APRICOT AND RAISIN STUFFING

Ideal for vegetarians

Ingredients

100g Dried apricots, chopped
100g Seedless raisins
350g White breadcrumbs, crusts removed
150g Butter, melted
1 Teaspoon salt
175g Celery, diced
A few knobs of butter

Method

1– Place the apricots and raisins into a bowl with enough water to cover them and bring to the boil. Strain then set aside.

2– Put the breadcrumbs into a bowl and pour the melted butter over.

3– Add the apricots, raisins, salt and celery to the breadcrumbs and mix well.

4– Place the stuffing either inside the bird to be roasted, or preferred, place into a greased oven tray, top with dots of butter and cover with foil. Bake for 1 hour in a hot (200 °C/400 °F/gas 6) oven.

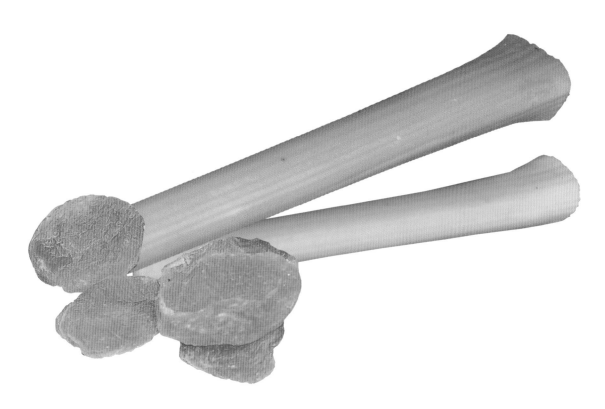

SAGE AND ONION STUFFING

Makes 6

Ingredients

2 Tablespoons of oil
1 Large onion, peeled and finely
   chopped
250g Sausage meat
2 Tablespoons fresh sage
   leaves, chopped
60g White breadcrumbs, crusts
   removed
Salt and freshly ground black
   pepper
A few knobs of butter

Method

1– Heat the oil in a pan and add the onion. Cook until soft and just turning colour. Take off the heat and transfer to a bowl to cool.

2– Add the sausage meat, sage and breadcrumbs to the onion, mix well, season then place either inside the bird to be roasted, or preferred, roll into balls and place on a greased oven tray. Top with dots of butter and cover with foil.

3– Bake for 45 minutes in a hot (200 ℃/400 ℉/gas 6) oven.

MAYONNAISE

Ingredients

1 Tablespoon Olive oil
2 Teaspoons Dijon Mustard
2 Egg yolks
300ml Olive oil
2 Teaspoons white wine vinegar
    (for lemon mayonnaise replace
    the vinegar with lemon juice)
Seasoning

Method

1– Place the one tablespoon of oil into a processor together with the mustard and egg yolks. Process until mixed. Alternatively, mix together thoroughly, with a whisk.

2– Very slowly, add the 300ml of olive oil. Do not rush this process otherwise your mayonnaise will curdle.

3– When all of the oil is combined, add the vinegar or lemon juice, seasoning and whisk to combine.

Seal and chill until needed.

POMMES PARMENTIER

Serves 4

Don't be put off by the title! Pommes parmentier is a dish of cubed potatoes, fried and served. This way of preparing potatoes is very easy, yet a good accompaniment to most dishes.

Ingredients

4 Tablespoons of olive oil
4 Large potatoes, peeled and
diced to approx 2cm square
1 Garlic clove, crushed
1 Small onion, chopped
3 Teaspoons breadcrumbs
Seasoning
½ Lemon

Method

1– Heat the butter and oil in a pan and add the cubed
potato garlic and onion. Cook, stirring occasionally,
until the potatoes are cooked and brown approximately
15–20 minutes.

2– Place the breadcrumbs on a tray and grill until they
become golden.

3– Place the breadcrumbs and seasoning into a bowl,
add the potatoes and mix gently. Serve with a squeeze
of lemon juice.

CRISPY ROAST POTATOES

Roast potatoes are always a crowd pleaser! To produce a perfectly crisp on the outside, fluffy on the inside, roasted potato, just follow these few simple rules and you will never fail. If you roast the potatoes whole; they will steam on the inside as the hot oil will seal them. Don't throw away the potato skins deep fry them and serve hot, with a tasty dip.

If you want to prepare the potatoes earlier than needed peel then place them in a bowl of cold water with a little lemon juice. Make sure that the potatoes are completely covered otherwise they will discolour.

If you wish to add a golden tint to the potatoes, add a few strands of saffron to the water when you are boiling them.

Ingredients

Allow two large potatoes per person

Cooking oil, to generously cover the bottom of a very strong roasting tin.

Method

Pre-heat oven 180 °C/350 °F/gas 4.

1– Peel the potatoes and leave whole.

2– Put the peeled potatoes in a large saucepan and cover with boiling salted water, simmer for approximately 15 minutes.

3– Meanwhile, put the oil in the roasting tin and place in a hot oven.

4– When the potatoes have become soft on the outside, drain well.

5– Return the potatoes to the saucepan and with the lid on, shake vigorously until the outside of the potatoes have become fluffy.

6– Bring the roasting tin of hot oil out of the oven and place on the top of the hob. Keep the oil very hot, remembering to take care.

7– Carefully place the potatoes into the very hot oil, then spoon the oil over each potato until they are completely coated.

8– Place the potatoes into the oven for approximately 80 minutes (depending on size) until they are crisp and golden.

Season with coarse milled rock salt and serve.

WHITE STAR
LINE.

TRIPLE-SCREW S.S. "REGINA."
16,500 TONS.

Hands Across the Sea

WHITE STAR LINE
TWIN-SCREW S S. "DORIC."

NAPKIN FOLDING

OPEN FAN NAPKIN page 126

CANDLE NAPKIN page 128

TIED FAN NAPKIN page 130

OPEN FAN NAPKIN

1– Start with a flat square napkin and fold the left hand side over to the right.

2–.From the bottom of the napkin; start to fold the halved napkin in a concertina pleat, leaving one third of the napkin unpleated.

3– Carefully turn the napkin over making sure that you hold the pleats tight then fold the napkin in half from right to left.

4– Fold the unpleated part of the napkin into a triangle.

5– Stand the napkin up along the edge of the triangle pleat.

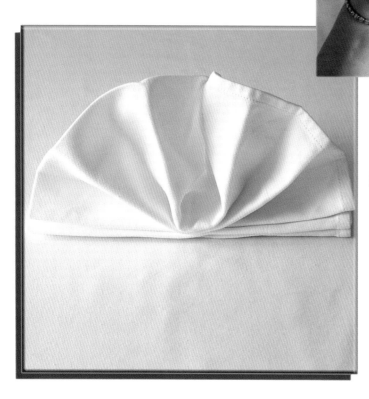

6– Let go of the pleats and they should fall down into a fan.

CANDLE NAPKIN

1– Start with a square flat napkin and fold the bottom right hand corner point not quite up to the top left point of the napkin.

2– Fold the bottom edge over once.

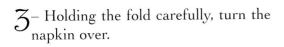

3– Holding the fold carefully, turn the napkin over.

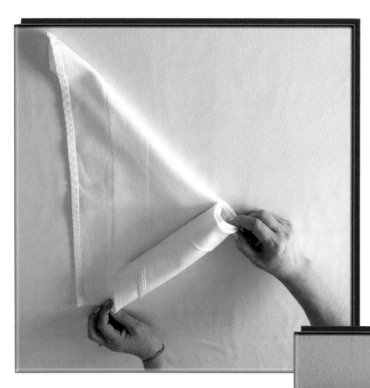

4– Roll the napkin up along the widest part of the fold.

5– Tuck the edge into the bottom fold.

6– Your napkin should now stand up in the shape of a candle.

TIED FAN NAPKIN

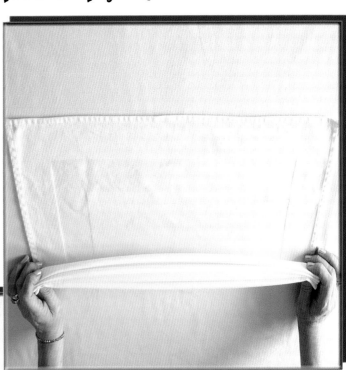

1– Start with a flat square napkin and concertina pleat from the bottom edge.

2– Continue to pleat the napkin right up to the top edge.

3– Fold the pleats in half.

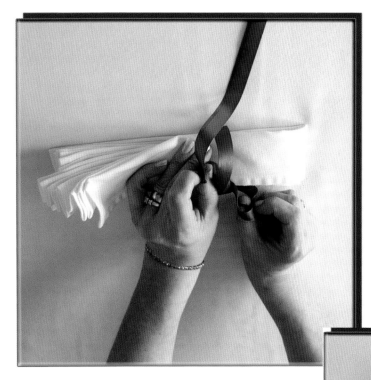

4.– Tie a ribbon to secure the pleated napkin in half.

5 – Lay the napkin on its edge with the bow facing you.

6 – Fan the top of the napkin out.

WHITE STAR LINE.

TRIPLE-SCREW S.S. "PITTSBURGH," 16,322 TONS.

Hands Across the Sea

WHITE STAR LINE

R.M.S. "OCEANIC" LEAVING NEW YORK.

CONVERSION TABLES

WHITE STAR LINE.

"OCEANIC HOUSE"

LONDON WEST END OFFICES.

Oven Temperature

°Celsius	°Farenheit	gas mark
110	225	gas mark ½
120	250	gas mark ½
130	275	gas mark 1
150	300	gas mark 2
160	325	gas mark 3
180	350	gas mark 4
190	375	gas mark 5
200	400	gas mark 6
220	425	gas mark 7
230	450	gas mark 8
240	475	gas mark 9

Weight

¼ oz	7g	9 oz	250g
½ oz	10g	10 oz	275g
¾ oz	20g	10 ½ oz	300g
1 oz	25g	11 oz	310g
1 ½ oz	40g	11 ½ oz	325g
2 oz	50g	12 oz	350g
2 ½ oz	60g	13 oz	375g
3 oz	75g	14 oz	400g
3 ½ oz	100g	15 oz	425g
4 oz	110g	1 lb	450g
4 ½ oz	125g	18 oz	500g ½ kg
5 ½ oz	150g	1 ¼ lb	600g
6 oz	175g	1 ½ lb	700g
7 oz	200g	1lb 10 oz	800g
8 oz	225g	2 lb	900g

Liquid

1 teaspoon	5ml	8fl oz	200ml
1 dessertspoon	10ml	9fl oz	225ml
1fl oz	15ml	10fl oz or ½ pint	250ml
1 ½ fl oz	30ml	11fl oz	300ml
2fl oz	40ml	12fl oz	325ml
2 ½ fl oz	50ml	13fl oz	350ml
3fl oz	60ml	14fl oz	370ml
3 ½ fl oz	75ml	15fl oz or ¾ pint	400ml
4fl oz	100ml	16fl oz	425ml
5fl oz or ¼ pint	125ml	17fl oz	450ml
5 ½ fl oz	150ml	18fl oz	500ml
6fl oz	160ml	19fl oz	550ml
7fl oz	175ml	20fl oz or 1 pint	600ml

American Cups

dry measures with approximate weights

FLOUR GRATED CHEESE ICING SUGAR	1 CUP 1 CUP 1 CUP	125g / 5oz
RICE - (UNCOOKED) RICE - (COOKED)	1 CUP 1 CUP	200g / 6.5oz 185g / 6oz
SUGAR - CASTER & GRANULATED	1 CUP	250g / 8 oz

liquid measures

¼ CUP	60ml	2 fl oz
⅓ CUP	80ml	2 ½ fl oz
½ CUP	120ml	4 fl oz
¾ CUP	180ml	6 fl oz
1 CUP	240ml	8 fl oz

Index